DELAWARE STATUTORY TRUSTS

THE DST

REVOLUTION

1031 EXCHANGE INTO RETIREMENT MODE

DON MEREDITH
DST·PIONEER

WITH JAMES BENES
40 YEARS W/CBS NEWS RADIO

WORD ASSOCIATION PUBLISHERS
www.wordassociation.com
1.800.827.7903

Printed in the United States of America.

ISBN: 978-1-63385-260-0

Designed and published by

Word Association Publishers
205 Fifth Avenue
Tarentum, Pennsylvania 15084

www.wordassociation.com

1.800.827.7903

Acknowledgments

I wish to thank first, my wife Brenda for endless hours despite her full-time responsibilities at General Dynamics NASSCO.

I need to thank Charles Jensen from Inland Realty Group for his guidance and support early on in this project. For chasing down the founders to arrange interviews. Including a conference call to the founders, who happened to be in a limo with the NAR president from Illinois outside the gate of the White House waiting for a meeting with the Vice President.

A big thank you to Geoff Flahardy, one of the early pioneers and rocks of this industry!

I have to thank James Benes, Mr. Chicago, formerly CBS NewsRadio forty-years, for his guidance and editing and his great interviews with the founders and president of Inland.

And lastly, I'd like to give a special thanks to former PricewaterhouseCooper corporate auditor & CPA Mark Kosanke. Mark is the original pioneer and voice of the entire DST industry, and he is the busiest guy I know.

TABLE OF CONTENTS

REVOLUTION FOR INCOME PROPERTY INVESTORS

"Owning an apartment complex straddles the line between an investment and a career." So wrote Steve Lander on Chron.com.

For many income property investors approaching or at retirement, the career part of that equation may no longer be as appealing. Here's where I need you to listen very carefully. If you knew what I know about DSTs, you likely would be scrambling to list your investment property without any delay. The benefits to you are startling, and the end of any tenants calling and bothering you are nearer than you think.

I have been working with investment property owners for twenty-plus years. I have been awed by them and amazed by them. I have learned from them and have been honored to collaborate with them.

While many others spend their time trying to figure out how to get wealthy in the stock market through short-term trading that often turns out to be somewhat painful, the investment property owner-warriors are showing what good old-fashioned hard work and patience can do for accumulating real wealth!

Investing in appreciating assets that generate income: what a concept! Many investors can make a good case by the numbers for owning property forever, especially in the area where I have lived for 28 years--San Diego. But we all get older and have retirement goals and travel plans, or we may have health issues to consider. Many in this hard-working class find they need hip and knee replacements. Some lives just change; perhaps unforeseen family issues now consume more of their time and don't seem so temporary.

The value of the property has appreciated. Maybe now is the time to pull the trigger and put that equity to work without being involved in the day-to-day management.

Is it time to fully immerse into retirement mode? What would life be like if you cleared the table of any responsibilities of active management? As one who became an accomplished oil painter and stage actor later in life, I can tell you there is life other than work! A 1031 exchange into a DST can deliver you there in a New York minute. [For a thorough definition of 1031 Exchange, jump to the chapter "Accommodators Perspective" with William Exeter.]

For some, the constant drumbeat for repairs, complaints about neighbors, concerns about capital maintenance, even frivolous litigations can take their toll over the years. For others the idea of selling properties they have known for years is like saying goodbye to a close family member. Realistically perhaps, they are no longer as enthusiastic about owning and managing the property as they once were.

Is there an exit strategy that makes sense? A strategy that I can get my hands around? Can I fully utilize the equity I have accumulated and deploy it to maximize monthly income? And dare I think it, never have another phone call or email from a tenant? Well, there is.

Welcome to the Delaware Statutory Trust: the "DST" as its more commonly referred to. And not to be confused with a deferred sales trust which also goes by DST, which I am no fan of for more reasons than I'm going to list here. Much has been written about the Delaware Statutory Trust as a 1031 Exchange. And for our readers who are attorneys and CPA's yes please note 2004-86 IRS Revenue ruling. Now let me direct you to an article posted by one of the largest 1031 escrow companies in the country about DSTs. Why? Because there's a lot I can say about DSTs and will (as well as others) as the book continues, but I wanted you to hear form a complete unbiased source. IPX Investment Property 1031 Exchange Services, Inc: A Subsidiary of Fidelity National Financial, a Fortune 500 Company. IPX wrote a detailed blog on their web site, "DSTs--An Option to Keep on your 1031 radar." This struck me as quite significant, as typically IPX doesn't often wander this close to endorsing any particular strategy from a specific industry. Considering all the research that a large institution puts into their content, I thought the endorsement signaled that DSTs had arrived and now were widely accepted as the highest standard for a 1031 Exchange.

Let me share some of what was posted:

> *"DSTs offer an intriguing option for investors who are looking for properties to complete their 1031 Exchanges.*
>
> *A DST (Delaware Statutory Trust) is an "arm chair investment", or a passive investment opportunity that allows individuals to own fractional shares in institutional grade properties. A DST is a legal entity created as a trust under Delaware law that can hold real estate. In the context of real estate, DSTs are formed pursuant to private governing agreements under which a property or several properties are held, managed, administered, and/or operated for profit by a trustee for the benefit of the holders of the DST's beneficial interests. Some examples of properties that were recently structured as DSTs are:*
>
> 1. *A portfolio of 17 storage properties in three states*
>
> 2. *An office building in Manhattan*
>
> 3. *A multi-family portfolio in Colorado*
>
> 4. *A large retail shopping center in California*

5. A portfolio of CVS and Walgreens stores located in Southern states

How does a DST work? A trustee of the DST initially purchases the property and takes title. The sponsor of the DST, the party who typically arranges the bank financing and coordinates the management of the property, then structures the transaction and arranges for sale of beneficial interests to individual investors. Though the beneficial interests are considered to be securities under federal securities laws, for purposes of 1031 Exchanges, Revenue Ruling 2004-86 states that a beneficial interest in a DST is considered "like-kind" real estate.

According to DST proponents, these are some of the benefits of DST ownership:

1. DSTs can offer higher quality, investment-grade assets that are typically only available to large institutions

2. DSTs provide investors with current income

3. DST investors have no management or day-to-day operation responsibilities

4. The debt is non-recourse, which means that in the event of a default, the DST investor is not personally liable

Of course, DSTs are not suited for all. Investors who enjoy managing the day-to-day operations of their properties may not be good *candidates. A DST is also not for an investor who wishes to invest in property for a short period since DST investments are typically designed for a holding period of two years or more. Additionally, DSTs are designed for "accredited investors" which are high net worth individuals as defined in Regulation D of the Securities Act of 1933.*

Given the intricacies of purchasing suitable real estate assets and structuring these offerings, from both a securities and tax perspective, exchangers and their advisors should perform due diligence when selecting a DST sponsor. The sponsor will provide a Private Placement Memorandum ("PPM") which provides information about the properties, area demographics, leases, projections and other important disclosures. Due diligence emphasis should be placed on real estate, property management and asset management expertise, prior performance track record, experience with sophisticated financing structures, transparent investor communications, financial strength of the sponsor and excellent legal representation."

DSTs have risks like all real estate and carry fees and expenses which may offset the benefits of tax deferral.

Ok, so there you have a good look at what some serious unbiased research is stating and a pretty respectable disclosure also. I will tell you 80% of what I am seeing are multi-family residential DSTs 300 to 400 units. And if you get the chance you will likely be impressed at the high level of management and software sophistication used to keep these properties operational. Their algorithms measure and track every bit of data both on site and off on a daily basis. And while we're at it, investors get these monthly reports of all the tracking data as well a quarterly management and budget reports. It is a very transparent process.

Having worked with investment property owners for years, I have seen many transformations from active manager to passive investor. I have heard all the wonderful stories and new pursuits that come with freeing up more time and letting go of--at least for a few--some serious stress. At some point owning investment properties can start to deplete your energy, or at the very least, interfere with fully immersing into retirement mode. For others, listing and selling properties and executing a 1031 Exchange into a DST investment grade property is simply a matter of taking advantage of a greatly appreciated property. Putting all that equity to work along with diversifying geographically and by asset class often also increases monthly income.

REALTORS:
THE BABY BOOMERS ARE COMING!

The leading edge of the baby boomers are, as of this writing, seventy-three years old. In many counties across the US, 30% of condos and residential property are owned as investment property, and in large part owned by this leading-edge baby boomer group. The number one question I get from income property owners is, "Why doesn't my realtor know about this?" While realtors are in the business of buying and selling properties, DST investing is outside of their licensing and expertise. More and more, investors expect realtors to collaborate and be familiar with strategies and solutions that are in the best interest of the client.

So, my question to realtors is, "What are you saying to this huge group of investors and income property owners?" This is a formidable group of income property owners who want out of managing tenants and the headaches that come with it. This group of boomers is heading into full blown retirement mode. So, at a time when listings are harder to come by, and the low hanging fruit for the most part is long gone, it is, as some realtors have discovered, wise to get into the planning mode and have a few strategies to put on the table. Becoming a bit familiar with the DST as a 1031 Exchange can bring real solutions and create an abundance of listings.

ACTUAL STORIES:

A realtor came to me who had nine properties. She had recently been diagnosed with a brain tumor on top of her many other health problems. She had concerns about leaving her husband with these properties; he had no experience in management, fixing things, or dealing with tenants. "He's absolutely helpless," she said. She now has reduced her actively managed properties to four and has exchanged the other five for DSTs. She is so happy with the strategy she has often sent out blogs and e-mails to every realtor she knows, "I can't believe you are all not incorporating this DST strategy to create listings. There are so many investment property owners out there in my shoes."

Then there's Diane and her Mom. They had owned about a dozen units in a building for around thirty-five years. The property was aging, and it was two hours away, depending of course on traffic. Calls from tenants regarding problems in the building--plumbing, electrical, the usual stuff and occasionally not so usual--were becoming more frequent--making life more stressful. She and her mother had been at this for decades, but Diane had just remarried, and these issues revealed themselves as an early disruption in the marriage relationship.

When she heard about the DST solution, Diane jumped into immediate research mode and after two meetings and getting answers to two pages of questions, she pulled the trigger, listed and sold her property for top dollar. She executed her first 1031 Exchange into three DST properties. Three years later she smiles as she recalls the transactions. She said, "I'll never forget returning from a one-week cruise, coming into the kitchen to see my answering machine actually not even blinking.... No calls. Not even one. *Sigh.*"

Ted and Louise owned nineteen properties, for which Ted loved to be a hands-on manager. But he was getting up in years and starting to become forgetful. Louise is fifteen years younger, and she had long worried about what would happen when Ted leaves this world. She would be staring down the barrel of nineteen properties. She argued that Ted was obsessed with the properties, and that they owned him, rather than the other way around. She went on to say that when you think about it, just to sell one property can be an ordeal. She would have to find a realtor, agree on listing parameters, show the property, accept an offer, go through the inspection process, respond to the list of inspection requests, and after all that, you often fall out of the first escrow. Doing a 1031 Exchange into DSTs reduces all this activity into a controllable, easily transferable asset that requires no day-to-day management. And no--as I like to call them-- "accidental owners." That is, a beneficiary who does not have the desire or wherewithal to take on the management of the investment properties.

For many owners of investment properties, it is situations like these that prompt owners to start thinking about an exit strategy. The DST 1031 Exchange is an effective way do that while deferring taxes. And you can continue to do the 1031 Exchange forever. "Swap till you drop" is what they say in the industry. Not sure how that sounds, but there it is.

Many investment property owners are familiar with 1031 Exchanges. That's the nickname given to Section 1031 of the U.S. Internal Revenue Service's tax code. The section provides that if an individual exchanges one investment property for another, he or she may be able to defer capital gains or losses they otherwise would have to deal with at the time of an outright sale.

It is not unusual however to run into investors who have sold their properties, closed escrow without opening a 1031 escrow account that links to the traditional escrow. They call me after the fact and ask about the DST. At this point it is too late. You are on your way to a substantial tax event unless, of course, you have some loss to offset this transaction. Many are stunned by the tax bill due in April. Some are prepared. Others try to make up for the lost income by investing in dividend stocks and bonds etc., only to find it will often take 10 years to break even from the tax loss, even if realizing a 5% return. The point here is, if you simply did a 1031 Exchange into a DST, often you would see your monthly income increase.

Back to our previous example. For Louise, getting Ted to gradually exchange property for DSTs was like trying to pry his fingers, one by one, from a vice grip. Ted, like many investment property owners, was a control freak who wants to be able to see, feel, and touch his property. Who can blame them? That's what has made them the successes that they are. To keep peace in the household, Louise has been getting him to lighten the load gradually, and they are both very pleased with the results. And as it so often happens, once all that appreciated equity goes to work in a DST property, you'll more than likely be collecting more monthly income than with the property you were actively managing. Plus, DSTs have deferred capital gains and renewed depreciation!

How Does a Delaware Statutory Trust (DST) Work?

A DST is a business trust created under Delaware law. It is a securitized investment that must comply with IRS Revenue Ruling 2004-86.

It allows investors to hold fractional shares in institutional grade properties. The properties are managed and administered by a trustee for the financial benefit of the investor. Yes, an investor can come in with all cash to invest in a DST, but most common are the 1031 Exchange investors. Cash or Exchange, or a combination, the investor gets the monthly income plus the income property tax advantages—more on that later.

In the examples above, Diane and her Mom and Louise and Ted became the "beneficial owners" of a DST. They sold their properties through a traditional residential or commercial real estate broker, but under a 1031 Exchange escrow contract.

Even before the sale, the investors began working with me, a DST investment professional. As your specialized DST investment rep, I follow the process, from listing to escrow close date; through all the moving parts to the 1031 Exchange escrow and finally to the selected DST property, making sure the investor's education is aligned with where we are in the process.

For some, our meeting is very transactional; for others there are financial planning discussions and strategies that need to take place to ensure that their goals, not only for income, but also for future liquidity and life concerns are all working together. There is a whole discovery process which concludes with a determination of best fit for the investor.

There may be future health care issues or long-term care needs. Concerns such as trust considerations, children, and any other issues that need to be discussed can be put on the table. With all this in mind, I keep you abreast of how your appreciated equity from your relinquished property (now in the 1031 escrow account) will be transferred into a DST.

As representative, along with the investor, we are working with very important time line rules. I am in constant communication with escrow and keep track of two deadlines the seller-now investor faces: 45 calendar days from the closing of the sale of the relinquished property to the identification of potential DSTs in which to invest, and 180 days from the closing of the sale to complete the acquisition of the new property. Figure 1 is a visual of this process.

Selecting potential DST investments is an interesting part of the process. The DST property may include

Figure 1: DST Basic Process Chart

multi-family units of two or three hundred units, or it could be healthcare-related office buildings, self-storage facilities, or triple net long term corporate leases like a Walgreens or a Napa Auto Parts or any number of companies. [In case the term is unfamiliar, a triple net lease is a **lease** in which the lessee pays rent to the lessor, as well as all taxes, insurance, and maintenance expenses that arise from the use of the property.] Right now, large multi-family residential complexes, 300 plus units, are a popular DST choice. I am always fascinated to listen to the acquisition guys talk about the selection process; they are the best in the business out there. And yes, the Amazon Effect is always out there in every discussion. [The Amazon Effect is the ongoing evolution and disruption of the retail market, both online and in physical outlets, resulting from increased e-commerce. The major manifestation of the Amazon Effect is the ongoing consumer shift to shopping online. ~Definition according to Whatis.com.] But, people will always need a place to live, and most people will stop by a local store for routine small things that they need, or at least the sundry or fresh items that missed the bulk buy list.

As a specialist in the DST industry, I am in constant contact with the capital corporations that are offering, or sponsoring, DSTs. Due diligence on my part ensures that only vetted sponsors are brought to the table for investor consideration. Well-capitalized, highly ethical, proven sponsors. These sponsors, as they are called, arrange for the trustees who manage the day-to-day operations of the properties. It is up to me to carefully monitor the equity available in each DST and to follow the pipeline as it relates to various escrow target close dates.

They say that when one does something frequently, one probably does it better! Every few months I walk into a mess where a well-meaning financial advisor stated enthusiastically, "Sure I can do DSTs." I can tell you as one who responds 24/7 to the many emails and calls from escrow, realtors, the investors' constant communication, the DST sponsors, their title and closing departments, and the 1031 Exchange point of contact, you have to be on the pulse of all these transactions. It is not unusual that I will encounter an investor's last-minute call to find out the uninformed financial advisor has his client thinking they're all set to close in three different DSTs. Then to find they are completely sold out and they are no longer a candidate to qualify for identification purposes under the forty-five-day rule. The transaction flow of escrow, 1031 Exchange and the language of the income property investor and the demands of the new DST property closing department is usually totally foreign to most financial advisors. It gets back to that adage what one does frequently, one tends to do better.

Unfortunately, those who claim to do DSTs have done one or no actual DST transactions. Many of these advisors have no clue or are totally out the loop in this industry--it is just outside their purview. OK, moving on.

THE STRENGTH OF A DST SOLUTION

In the eyes of the IRS, a beneficent interest in a DST is considered a direct interest in real estate. The owner of that interest has the right to receive distributions from rental income or the sale of the property. But the owner does not have the responsibilities of property management. The owner-investor has a purely passive relationship to the trust's properties.

The owner-investor does not have title to the property, so he/she does not have liability, the loan is non-recourse to you. This is in contrast to TIC (Tenant-In-Common) structures which were popular in the 1990s and in the early 2000s before the start of the 2008 recession.

Because the DST is not considered a taxable entity, all profits are passed through to the investor. But note, as with any business operation, profits are not guaranteed, and losses may also be passed to the investor. (Inland Private Capital Corporation is the giant in the DST market. It has 40 percent of market share and 50 years of experience.)

Because of size, DSTs can offer investors a chance to place equity into large-scale, high quality portfolios that are usually available only to institutional investors.

If the DST seeks to finance a project, the loan is negotiated by the DST. There is no need for owner-investors to be qualified as borrowers. Their credit rating remains unchanged.

There is no term limit for the signatory trustee of the DST. This should give the investor the comfort of a continuing management of the property.

This really gets exciting in the last chapter "Saved the Best for Last" with Mark Kosanke.

LIMITS ON THE POWER OF A DST TRUSTEE

They're known as the "Seven Deadly Sins." They are limits set on the power of a DST trustee by IRS ruling 2004-86.

So we mentioned the IRS ruling 2084-86; so what's that all about? OK, —Here it is:

1. Once the offering is closed, there can be no future capital contributions to the DST by either current or new beneficiaries. To allow further contributions would dilute the original investors' percentages of ownership.

2. The trustee cannot renegotiate the terms of any existing mortgage loans, nor can it obtain any new mortgage financing from any party except

when a property tenant is bankrupt or insolvent. If a trustee were allowed to assume greater liabilities (and thus increase risk), it would be doing so without the consent, and possibly to the dissatisfaction, of the beneficiaries.

3. The trustee cannot enter into new leases or renegotiate existing leases except when a property tenant is bankrupt or insolvent. DSTs operate best when their invested properties are under long-term leases to credit-worthy tenants. These types of leases mean the investment will be more secure.

4. The trustee cannot reinvest the proceeds from the sale of its real estate. The IRS ruling requires that all proceeds from a DST investment should be distributed to investors. It is they who have the right to determine how to reinvest the capital.

5. The trustee is limited to making the following types of capital expenditures with respect to the property: (a) expenditures for normal repair and maintenance of the property; (b) expenditures for minor non-structural capital improvements of the property, and (c) expenditures for repairs or improvements required by law. The trustee cannot make a major upgrade to the property, such as adding new units to a complex or building a clubhouse; there is no assurance that costs for this would be recouped at the time of sale. Less major value-added upgrades like upgrading apartment

interiors or adding a dog park or a fitness center are permissible.

6. All cash, other than necessary reserves, must be distributed to the investors on a current basis. DST trustees are allowed to keep a reserve of cash for repairs or other unexpected expenses. They are required, however, to make distributions to beneficiaries within the expected time frame.

7. Any cash held between distribution dates can only be invested in short-term debt obligations. A short-term debt is considered the equivalent of cash because it can be readily re-converted to cash for distribution to investors. So now that I've listed all these I'll tell you the sponsors that offer the DST property are as you can well imagine are all over these points so not to worry! OK, let's move on.

In a worst-case scenario, that of a DST violating one of these restrictions despite the best intentions of the trustee, the state of Delaware allows the DST to convert into a Limited Liability Company. This is a safety net to protect investors. An LLC is a business entity that can be taxed like a partnership, but it protects its shareholders from liability beyond their investment.

So, these 'Seven Deadly Sins" are, in reality, aimed at providing protections for the investors.

ANOTHER EXAMPLE OF MORE TYPICAL DISCLOSURES

A DST is a securities product with real estate at its core. These are some of the factors a would-be investor should consider:

- DSTs may not be suitable for investors who want to continue managing their properties.

- DSTs may not be suitable for those seeking only a short-term investment. DSTs are designed for a holding period of two years or more.

- DSTs have risks like all real estate, are illiquid, and have fees and expenses associated with the purchase, which may offset some of the benefits of the tax deferral of the 1031 exchange.

- DSTs are designed for "accredited investors," individuals of high net worth or income level, as defined by Regulation D of the Securities Act of 1933. At the time of this writing, this equates to a net worth of over one million not including principal residence, or an annual income of $200,000 (or $300,000 combined with spouse) for the last two years and expected in the next.

- Because of the complexities of selecting and structuring real estate offerings, would-be investors and their registered representative need to exercise due diligence in choosing a DST sponsor. The sponsor will provide a Private Placement Memorandum (PPM). This provides information about the properties, such as area demographics, leases, and projections.

- The investor and the registered representative should consider a sponsor's expertise at property and asset management, the sponsor's track record, the sponsor's experience with sophisticated financing structures, its financial strength and legal representation, and the transparency of its communication with investors.

- The investor should remember that real estate is subject to the cycles of the economy, just like other investments. The value of a property may fall because of factors such as variations in occupancy, oversupply of space in an area, increases in operating costs, tenant defaults, adverse changes in laws, etc.

- There is no guarantee that investment objectives will be achieved.

Getting Started

You won't see notices of any public offerings of DSTs or any advertisements promoting them. Because of Securities and Exchange Commission rules, DST securities are usually offered to a select group of a relatively small number of investors.

This means that to get into the market, you've got to find a qualified registered representative to manage the transition from the sale of your property with equity going into a 1031 escrow account, to finding the right DST sponsor, and making sure all the paperwork is in order.

Around the country, there is a core of investment professionals who can do this for you. DSTs are the only thing I do, and I've been doing them for 18 years. I am in constant communication with the internal staffs at these various DST real estate sponsors. They brief me daily on equity available for our investors in a DST property, and they assist in answering the intricate questions from the investor about various aspects of the programs.

We want to educate the investor and more importantly make sure this is a good fit: to explain DST rules and how the investment will work. Some investors prefer to do more of their own research and educate themselves. Some ask good questions, but not necessarily the right questions. So, I share my many years of transactional experience with them.

You have to understand, many of these investors have owned property for 30, 40, or even 50 years. They know their own property inside and out: every electrical outlet, plumbing fixture, roofing improvement, sidewalk, garage, every last detail. It may be difficult for them to even contemplate ceding control of their property. Did I say difficult? Well, that's an understatement, right?

Of course, for others with business acumen, the emotions don't come into play. The math simply works out. The numbers line up: equity goes to work in a DST, monthly income continues, the tax write-offs are there, and the depreciation clock is re-set.

Through a DST, we are able to remove the burden of management and repairs, trading the investor's hard-earned equity for a 1031 Exchange into DST equity shares in institutional grade properties.

Take the case of a retired doctor. He boasted that his advisor was setting up his $3 million equity in six DSTs. A look at the paperwork, however, indicated that half of those DSTs had already been sold out. His advisor hadn't paid close enough attention, and the investment went sour.

For those of us who work exclusively with DSTs, the number one rule is what they teach at Harvard Medical School: Do no harm!

For many others, that just doesn't apply.

DO NO HARM

As they say in Harvard Medical School, "Do no harm." As an investment professional, I am a specialist with a focus on the 1031 Exchange area of real estate as it relates to DST income real-estate. In fact, you might even say I am a pioneer in the industry, as you would be hard-pressed to find anyone who has done an exchange into a DST before me.

That being said, I have an obligation to my clients to consider their entire portfolio of investments, and to advise them if I think DSTs may not be in their best interests. I recently advised an investor after a lengthy meeting to consider an Airbnb for one of his properties. For him, his life circumstances and the location of his properties all wrapped together; that was a good option I thought he should have on the table. In this particular case, the investor was 52 years old, and he had a successful restaurant that was on auto pilot. He had nothing but time on his hands during the week and seemed to be looking for a project at this time in his life. I introduced him to a friend of mine who shared her recent experiences with the Airbnb model. A year later he is still perfecting his Airbnb property, but he also decided to do a 1031 Exchange into a DST with one of his other properties that did not have a good cash flow.

If an investor is coming out of one property, he or she has the opportunity to diversify into two or three DSTs, diversifying by not only asset type, but also geographically as well.

Even in a real estate portfolio, it is prudent to have diversification. The best bet is to have a mix, a variety of holdings.

Let's turn now to what is, perhaps, the prime motivator of 1031 Exchanges and DSTs: deferring capital gains taxes. In a conversation with Geoff Flahardy, one of the pioneers of the industry and one of my favorite go-to guys, he provided the following information.

"First, let's be sure about what capital gains are. Say you purchased a property a few years ago, and then made a lot of improvements to it. When you sell, the capital gain is the difference between the sales price minus the closing costs on the one hand, and what you paid for the property plus what you put into it on the other. The price you paid plus the cost of improvements is known as your cost basis.

If you have taken a loan on your property, that must be paid off at the time of sale, but it doesn't reduce your capital gain. The amount of this debt, however, as well as the equity you've received, can be transferred into a DST. The rules make the math work out that way.

In fact, under the rules for 1031 Exchanges, the new investment and any debt on the properties must be equal to or greater than the old. This is the government's way of encouraging new investments to stimulate the economy.

Most DSTs come packaged with a new loan, usually about 52% loan to value as it's called. The individual investor does not have to go through a loan process. The DST sponsor does that; the loan is secured by the property.

There are a number advantages to increasing equity and debt in a DST. The investment is larger and thus the possibility of growth in equity is larger. Value is also increased through debt with a higher loan-to-value. The investor is not responsible if the loan should default. That's the responsibility of the sponsor with the loan secured by the property." It should be noted that higher debt can also increase the risk in a property.

Let's take a closer look at the new debt and the new possible depreciation schedule, and what it will mean. Here's an example, prepared for us by Geoff Flarhardy, the national accounts director of ExchangeRight of Pasadena, California:

Relinquished Property Value: $1,000,000

*Adjusted Cost Basis: $0.00

Replacement Property Purchase Value: $2,000,000

Loan-to-Value: 50%

Surplus value acquired: $1,000,000

Land Value: 20% = $200,000 – You cannot depreciate land value.

Improvement Value = $800,000

Asset Class: Commercial – 39-year depreciation schedule

Cost recovery = $20,512.82 ($800,000 / 39)

If the DST is paying 6%, then $20,512,82 of the $60,000 of income would be sheltered, or 34.19%.

NOTE: This is just an example and should not be considered a model for tax purposes.

*Basis is the term for the cost of a property for tax purposes. It begins with the purchase price of the property and is increased as improvements are made but decreased for items such as depreciation. The difference between the sales price of the property and the adjusted basis will result in the figure for capital gains that are taxable.

HOW IT ALL STARTED FOR ME

I have been a registered representative since 1990 and spent most of those years managing stock and bond accounts. But real estate and related investments were really my passion. So, when a CPA, formerly of Pricewaterhouse, gave me a heads up that you could now do 1031 Exchanges into DSTs that really caught my attention.

I have always enjoyed and respected investors who owned, rehabbed and managed their properties. For me, that's much more satisfactory than engaging in experimenting with stock strategies to make short-term gains, which often fall short of expectations.

It has been much more rewarding utilizing 1031 Exchange strategies to help investors find exit strategies that will reduce their burdens and help them into a retirement in which they can enjoy the fruits of their many years' labors.

These investors are smart, they can do the math, and they have great intuition. My role is to put the facts on the table for them, and to answer their questions in what usually turns out to be a lengthy but satisfying due diligence process.

Typically, I do a lot of listening in my first contact with property owners. They can be in various stages of the process. Some are planning an exit strategy for two or three years in the future. Others have already listed their properties and started work on a 1031 Exchange. Regardless of where they are, my role is to listen, and to listen carefully. Why are they selling? Is it because of stress? Is income replacement a key issue? They may own several properties. They may just recently have heard about DSTs. Are they familiar with 1031 Exchanges?

From a financial planning viewpoint, I must listen on several levels.

I may have to explain what the 1031 Exchange process looks like, from closing to escrow to 1031 Exchange escrow to how the funds will be wired to the DST property.

There are so many other things to consider: what are their other investments? Their IRAs? Their 401Ks? How much liquidity do their investments have? Are their current land holdings in an LLC, an S corporation, or a trust? How much will they need in the future? Are there children to be concerned about? What about long-term care needs? What are their income requirements? Are they an accredited investor? Would a DST investment of five to seven years work for them? We have to talk about it all. As I write this I just got off the phone with my IT guy who owns several rental properties. He has been selling a few of them the last year and exchanging into DSTs. Talk about a guy who does research, leave it to an IT guy. Anyway, he just shocks me and says I have one last property just closing and then the wife and I are going on an extended world tour starting in Portugal! I have really been interested in Portugal the last few years. Why? because if you do any research on travel or ex-pats living abroad you will find countless sources such as Forbes, Trip Advisor, International Living Magazine all touting Portugal as one of the best destinations for Americans on the globe for numerous reasons. Safety, healthcare, cost of living, lifestyle and the list is endless… Anyway, why am I so surprised by them announcing their plan? Because I have known him and his wife for years and I swear all they ever did was work night and day! It's like where did this come from? Well, it's another example of a DST shouldering the load yet again. In this case it is freeing them up to actually pull this off. That's why I love this industry. Anyway, where was I?

For some, I have to do a lot of hand-holding. For others, who are business-savvy and transaction-oriented, not so much.

These days, we see investors with two to three-hundred thousand dollars to invest, or up into the millions. The investment can be solely from their relinquished investment property, or they can add additional cash to this new DST.

As DSTs have grown in acceptance and credibility over the years, the amounts going into them get larger and larger each year. Substantial investors, coming out of large commercial properties, may go into three or four different DSTs. The Inland Real Estate companies do special carve-outs for these large investors.

We are always learning more about these particular real estate companies and the DSTs they offer. Our collaboration will provide sound confidence for the investor's strategy moving forward.

THE FOUNDATION, TRUST AND INTEGRITY OF THIS INDUSTRY STARTED WITH INLAND

In my opinion the industry exists and has such a high standard of operation because of one great American company by the name of Inland Group of Real Estate Companies. It is the grandfather of the industry. Inland set the bar so high to begin with, their ethics and integrity are for all to follow. When talking about DSTs, the names of a few other real estate companies must be talked about in some detail. But I am going to focus mainly on The Inland Group of Real Estate Companies. And yes, there are others like ExchangeRight, and newcomer to the DST industry, the 80-year-old New York Bond company Cantor Fitzgerald. You may remember them from 9/11 as they lost many employees in the World Trade Center collapse. There are several others I could add to the list, but I have to start with what can only be called a great American story: the heralded, greatly admired for their ethics and investor-first reputation I'd like you to meet Inland.

THE INLAND REAL ESTATE COMPANIES

If there is a 600-pound gorilla in the DST industry, it is the Inland Group of Real Estate Companies. They have been around for 50 years. Inland's motto is "Good Deeds. Since 1968."The name Inland also is not only a play on words— "In Land," but it was chosen to reflect the idea that the whole company is more than the sum of its parts.

It was started by a group of school teachers, if you can imagine that. Now Inland stands out as the industry leader in creating, developing, and supporting real estate investment funds.

Inland companies have sponsored more than 700 investment programs for about half a million investors. Inland controls about 40 percent of the market.

Everything about Inland, its acquisition process, management style, and investor services, all of it is held to the highest ethical standard.

And that's what you might expect from a company that was founded by four Chicago public school teachers. The first people to invest in the company founded by Dan Goodwin, Bob Baum, Joe Cosenza and Bob Parks were also school teachers, or their own families and friends. Their founding notion was that real estate was a basic human need, and therefore a reliable investment stream.

Their motivation for starting Inland was the need to increase their income above the $6,000/year salary they got as teachers. They began by pooling their money, $100 here, $500 there, then building houses and small apartment buildings and opening a real estate brokerage. They did all of the work themselves: painting, decorating, and selling the properties. That took a lot of time, but in the early years they had it. They were free each day after 3:15 p.m., and then of course, there were weekends.

They were very successful. Very successful. Within five years, all four of them quit their teaching jobs to devote their full time to Inland.

About 10 years after its founding, Inland had 10,000 apartment units under its management for the company's limited partners. Each complex was a different partnership. Joe Cosenza, now with the title of Vice Chairman of The Inland Real Estate Group, LLC and President of Inland Real Estate Acquisitions, says he was able to drive to all of them. They were all in the Midwest, in Illinois, Wisconsin, and northern Indiana, not that very far from Chicago. Inland also owned related businesses, like construction, waste removal and pest control businesses.

By 1981, Inland reached a milestone, having collected $100 million in limited partnerships. By 1985, the company had 42,000 apartment units under management. That year, according to Cosenza: "We did one other thing that was new. And that was, we formed the first *public* limited partnership. All the rest of them had to have, like, 35 investors. You could expand that a little bit but that's all you could have. That's what the rules were, what the SEC rules were. So, we decided, why don't we, even though no one knows us around the country, why don't we do public limited partnerships so we could sell in every state and buy in every state then too. We did. It was very smart because we started to do it, and we did it without any more hitches on any of the properties."

But a big hitch in Inland's businesses came in 1986. That's when the Tax Reform Act removed many benefits from real estate investments, even retroactively. Cosenza calls it a "disaster" that sent real estate prices plummeting and literally crushed all savings-and-loans over the next few years. Without S&Ls, real estate companies had a tough time financing investment.

Developers couldn't finance improvements, and jobs were lost all across the board, from legal and financial services to the people who did construction, painting, carpeting and so forth.

Inland's response to this crisis is admirable and noteworthy. Cosenza again: "Toward the end of the '80s, 1988, '89, we did a couple of things. One, we had about 400 limited partnerships by then, but the bottom 10% weren't worth what they were when the investors went into them. So, the four of us took almost the whole year to figure out how we could save these people, because we couldn't live with anybody losing money with us. And so, we came up with a couple of ideas. The first idea was, if we could get with a public company and do a sale-leaseback to them on their real estate, and they were a healthy company, we could buy that. We could have the investors vote to sell the one that wasn't so good, and whatever money they had they could put into the new one, and we would put in the rest of the money out of our pockets."

That's how Inland became the landlord for Wal-Mart, in fact Wal-Mart's biggest landlord for the next 20 years. Cosenza says the deal cost the four partners $17 million, but "nobody lost money with us at the time, and we all (could) sleep well."

In the 1990s, Inland focused more on commercial properties like shopping centers, industrial properties, and vacant land suitable for development. In 1994, Inland formed its first Real Estate Investment Trust, or REIT (pronounced "Reet"). REITs became popular because they could be publicly sold on the New York Stock Exchange. They are modeled after mutual funds and each REIT can have thousands of investors.

Inland's first REIT contained 140 shopping centers. Inland decided to go into retail because the retail industry was on the upswing after a slump in the late 1980s. The second REIT came in 2000 and focused on properties in the South and all along the East Coast. The third REIT included properties in the West. In total, Inland has formed eight REITS with assets in the tens of billions of dollars.

When Inland began, its partnerships were formed as Illinois Land Trusts. That's all that was available. There could be multiple investors in a trust, and their identities were protected. Each investor could sell his/her share, and the lender holding the paper on the trust needn't give approval. The lenders liked the trusts because the trust was the title-holder and the signer of the mortgage.

In the 1990s, Cosenza became aware of something called the Delaware Business Trust. It was similar to an Illinois Land Trust, but it was available in all of the states. Inland got its team of lawyers to work on ways to structure a Delaware Business Trust like an Illinois Land Trust, and "after thousands and thousands of dollars of legal fees, sure enough, we could structure it to have multiple owners, and most importantly, you could structure it so that if an individual is inside this trust, he can sell his partnership interest in exchange for someone's deed. Or vice versa. In other words, if someone sells a property for deed, normally the IRS only agrees to a deed to deed for a 1031 Exchange, but here we had the ability to make a land trust and the beneficial interest in that land trust acts just like a deed, so that the person sold his deed could tax exchange his deed into the beneficial interest of that trust and it was OK by the IRS."

Voila! The Delaware Statutory Trust was born. Actually, in the year 2000, the state of Delaware made the name change from Business Trust to Statutory Trust.

You could call Joe Cosenza the "Father of the DST," but he is more modest, crediting Inland, the corporation, as the father. He does say, however, that Inland was, without a doubt, one of the forerunners in the industry.

In 2001, Inland formed its Private Capital Corporation for 1031 Exchange investors. It now has six billion dollars in assets. It has raised three billion from people who decided to sell their assets and exchange into a new deal. Cosenza explains:

"Now each Delaware Statutory Trust owns one building. Maybe it owns two buildings. But they're all separate on their own. And stand on their own. And in the course of the years… one of the things we did different than any other company was that we bought the assets first, we financed it first, inside that Delaware Statutory Trust so that when an investor saw the deal, it was already clean. It was already completed, and now they could exchange into it, without any worry that the deal may have fallen through, or that the loan was different from what they thought they saw on paper. We would never do that. Other companies did, and they caused disasters in the marketplace."

Inland has strict standards for its DST business and the properties it acquires: "it's got to be, of course, scrutinized left and right by Inland with due diligence, got to pass our due diligence standards, got to pass the standards of enough of a cash flow. It's got to pass the standards of a lender to lend against it. Usually we do 55% financing. Safe. When you're around the 50% level there's a lot of room there before you will ever get hurt. And then lastly, the due diligence is performed by broker-dealers, financial planners, who sell this. Now keep in mind, we've dealt with financial planners since the 1970s, some of which we're still dealing with. Anyhow, when you deal in that world, now you're dealing with securities. So now you have another threshold of due diligence. The broker-dealers do their due diligence with the financial planners, and you have to pay them for the cost of their due diligence. So, if they pass it, now you've got two complete sets of due diligence done. On the real estate level, the securities level, and the real estate level again… That's why we have 40 percent of the business across the country…We have very high standards."

It is not always a person who has sold property who wants to invest in a DST. About 30 percent of investors want to invest because of the cash flow. They may like a property being offered in a DST. Cosenza says he does that himself.

Lenders like DSTs for several reasons: a DST is a single entity, not the 100 or 200 or more people who are invested in it; lenders see DSTs as bankruptcy-remote; the lender has further security because the sponsor of the DST has a fiduciary responsibility; and there is one sponsor, one manager of the property.

The lengths of DSTs vary. They could be as short as two, three or four years, or even as long as ten. The length is determined by the marketplace. It is the sponsor, like Inland, who advises when it's time to sell, or when it's time not to sell.

As for the costs to investors, Cosenza explains: "All the fees are exposed. They have to be. From the day, we started doing business like that. First of all, you've got a broker-dealer who gets a fee, it's usually about six percent, and then you have to pay for their due diligence. They've got to do real estate and securities and that's about one and a quarter percent. And then you have ours which is about two to two and a half percent. And anything else, third party reports. You have to have an engineering report. You've got to know that bricks-and-mortar isn't sinking. You've got to know it's got no mold. You've got to know all this stuff because you might not be able to see it visually. Then you have to have an environmental report. You don't know what's in that ground…. Appraisal and lender fees. The lender might charge you half a point. All those fees are right there, upfront."

When the housing bubble crashed in 2008, Inland felt the pain. But it also saw the opportunity. Real estate prices dropped, and Inland responded by becoming the largest buyer of real estate in the nation.

As for the future, Cosenza doesn't foresee much change in the DST market unless Congress again acts to change the tax laws like it did in 1986. Cosenza points all the way back to 1921. That's when Congress first enacted like-kind exchange rules. The idea was to allow investors to trade up and those with lower income to get into the investment market in the first place. The idea was to encourage investment and grow the economy. It worked.

In the retail area, there's also something called "The Amazon Effect." Cosenza says "Amazon is a killer. They're murderers. They're slayers." He's talking about the negative consequences to retailers who are losing business to Amazon. But he says Amazon can't do everything. Inland is interested in places where people may go two or three times a week, like grocery stores. Or other businesses Amazon can't replace: like gas stations, cleaners, the local ice cream store, or the corner liquor store. Shopping centers with those kinds of businesses are located everywhere.

Cosenza and Inland are very proud of the commitment the company has made to the communities in which it operates. In 2009, the Better Business Bureau gave Inland its first Torch Award for Ethics in the Marketplace. Inland has won that award three times. The Chicago Association of Realtors has been honoring individuals with its Hall of Fame since 1883. In 2014, Inland became the first corporation to be so honored.

Inland is truly an American story. A company with an investor-first philosophy, Midwestern ethics. It's the heart and soul of America. What every company should be.

Cosenza himself is truly the product of the American Dream, his father's dream as well as his own. After Joe's father immigrated to the U.S. from Italy in 1922, he opened a barber shop in Chicago. In the late '20s, a bookie joint opened right across the street. Al Capone was the owner. Capone went to Joe's Dad for his haircuts.

Joe asked his Dad if he was afraid. He was, but he still cut the mobster's hair because Capone would tip $20 on a haircut that cost 25 cents. Joe's rise to be one of the chiefs of a great American corporation had to be his father's dream for his son.

Today Joe Cosenza remembers his father fondly, the lessons he taught, and Joe honors his Dad by having his old barber's chair installed in a corner of Joe's Inland office in Oak Brook, Illinois.

Al Capone Sat Here. Joe Cosenza's Father's Barber Chair.

INTERVIEW WITH KEITH LAMPI, PRESIDENT & CEO

The youthful president of Inland Private Capital majored in economics and minored in finance at the University of Illinois in Champaign. He says he was drawn to the financial markets and had a particular interest in real estate. He's been with Inland for 16 years:

"I took my first position at Inland kind of thinking to myself: this would be a good start, [it would] expose me to a number of things, and after a couple of months I was hooked. I realized it's so intuitive, such a dynamic asset type, one that isn't just a buy-hold-sell. It's a buy; it's a manage; it's a devote creativity-and-resources, navigating what's going on in the marketplace, what may occur, and how to deal with a lot of problem-solving. It's not a one-size-fits-all kind of proposition. There's so much going on that intrigued me that I realized real estate is where I belonged."

Tell us about the Great Recession of 2008, how that affected real estate in general and Inland in particular.

"Oh gosh, it was, from my perspective it was the first real economic downturn that I had personally faced, and that our industry had faced... The securitized 1031 market really didn't begin until the late '90s, early 2000s, and really wasn't big enough to speak to the economic volatility in the early 2000s. So, it really kind of established a footwork or foundation and grew incrementally, year over year."

"The IRS came out with guidance in 2002 that catapulted the growth of the industry. Then again in 2004 it further [enhanced] the legitimacy of the securitized 1031 market, and there was more or less vertical sales growth, demand drive from investors all the way up to about 2007, 2008. And the Great Recession hit."

"It was a recession that was deep-rooted. It was a real estate-related recession. It was a finance-related recession, and our industry all about went away. Commercial real estate broadly speaking was absolutely affected; everything was affected. There was a high degree of uncertainty early on. There were questions being asked with respect to, say are some of the major banks going to be nationalized? Concepts that are so fundamental to commercial real estate, there were such open-ended question marks. It was a scary time."

"A lot of sellers either weren't selling because they didn't like the value or weren't selling because they couldn't find a buyer willing to pay anything for their property; oftentimes the buyer couldn't finance it because there was so much uncertainty with respect to the banks. I'll say it was probably an 18-month period. We were on pretty shaky footing... Various incremental steps were taken throughout that built confidence and re-established the fact that we maybe kind of hit a bottom and were kind of coming out of that, and the industry by most accounts almost had to start over."

"I think sponsors like Inland were forced to take a hard look in the mirror and look at what we'd done pre-recession and we could do post. That is, create products that were better positioned to weather an economic downturn or storm. So, cost structures, fee structures were looked at in very, very critical fashion. What asset types were acquired on behalf of our broader marketplace from a sector and geography standpoint, and how to better provide investors with more diversity. All of these were questions we were asking ourselves as sponsors. Broker-dealers were asking themselves as the fiduciary on behalf of their investors, and as a result I actually think they came out better, stronger and in a better position to service their clientele."

Lampi says the industry is again on an upward trajectory, but the 2007-8 downturn is always in the back of one's mind. He says there's emphasis on putting investors in long-term vehicles that have the ability to weather an economic storm.

LONG-TERM MINDED. HOW LONG ARE WE TALKING ABOUT?

"I typically like our program built with a 10-year time horizon. Certainly, that could go longer. There are absolutely various examples I could cite where the holding period was shorter, depending on macroeconomic factors and what the general market was as related to opportunities or challenges. Ten years is typically what we model."

CAN YOU GIVE US SOME IDEA ABOUT THE ANALYTICS, THE SOFTWARE YOU USE TO EVALUATE A PROPERTY?

"I could go on a long-winded narrative about what technology has done for markets and pockets of industries. Real estate's no different. What technology has basically done, is it allows us to evaluate a larger volume of opportunities in a compressed, shorter period of time in a more thorough way.

"It's a game of numbers: the more you look at, the more opportunities you can unearth that make sense and fit the objective you ultimately want to provide investors. So, the more you can look at in a timely fashion, the better. That means from a demographic analysis standpoint, having access to technology that gives you profiles on certain markets as it relates to income and population growth and then all of the various factors you might want to see if you're buying an apartment complex, for example.

"But it doesn't stop there. There's a variety of different proprietary software systems that we'll invest in and we subscribe to that also give us intel in what the market rents are within a one-mile radius of the property we're going to acquire… How many units are being developed which may impact your ability to maintain your occupancy level or push rents. New job growth that's occurring in the area. The list goes on and on…"

IS THERE A TREND TOWARD MORE MULTI-FAMILY APARTMENTS?

"We're of the belief that the only way you're really going to make money in real estate on a near-term and even mid- and long-term basis if you're buying in this market environment is to purchase assets with operating characteristics. What that basically means is you want to buy assets that you believe you can create and add value to by rolling up your sleeves and being a solid manager of real estate by maximizing occupancy and rent growth on the income side of the equation, and shrewdly managing your expenses on the expense side of the equation. Imagine your tax increases, insurance, salaries, all the ancillary expenses that translate to your bottom line. Apartments fit that mold well. They're assets that don't manage themselves.

"Yes, it's important to buy a good asset in a well-located market but the story doesn't end there. You also have to be good at what you do in managing that asset on behalf of investors…creating that market value by being a shrewd asset manager. Apartments really accomplish that goal for us. And we also see some of the same opportunity in student housing and self-storage and other assets…"

IN THE LOBBY OF INLAND PRIVATE CAPITAL CORPORATION THERE ARE PHOTOGRAPHS OF SOME OF INLAND'S HOLDINGS, INCLUDING STUDENT HOUSING AT THE UNIVERSITY OF CENTRAL FLORIDA AND VARIOUS MEDICAL OFFICE BUILDINGS ALL ACROSS THE COUNTRY. WE ASKED: WHAT'S THE DIFFERENCE BETWEEN MEDICAL OFFICE BUILDINGS AND OTHER OFFICE BUILDINGS?

"The medical office arena is more of a planned demography. It's a more of a play on the healthcare sector. Corporate office space is a different animal… It's more downtown, centralized… A medical office can be successful in the surrounding suburban sprawl. Proximity to major hospital systems oftentimes play to the analysis in evaluating a medical practice that may house themselves sin a medical office building.

"But really, the medical office building or MOB sector is with the demographic trend of the Baby Boomers, the aging sector… This is a play on demography which just isn't really the same thought process when you're looking at corporate office space. In fact, there's some research in suggesting that there's more transient employees, there's more of a desire to provide employees with the option to work from home that would ultimately lessen the floor plan a corporate office may need, so it really is a pretty different analysis--when all is said and done."

PROPERTY OWNERS HAVE DIFFERENT OPTIONS IN CASHING OUT, INCLUDING CHARITABLE REMAINDER TRUSTS AND INSTALLMENT SALES AMONG OTHERS. ANY THOUGHTS?

"From a tax standpoint, clearly these are options; it's not a one-size-fits-all. Each investor has a different set of needs, desires, objectives that they aspire to accomplish. That's why it's so important for investors to work with a team of financial professionals, starting with the financial advisor… their accountants and estate planning attorneys and making sure that the decisions that are made fit within the broader objectives of the client's plan. I wouldn't sit here and suggest that one approach is better than another or makes sense …That's going to be ferreted out when a client steps back and works with a team of professionals."

ARE THERE LONG AND SHORT STRATEGIES FOR INVESTMENT PROPERTIES?

"I think there can be. I would say the securitized 1031 market has been more of a long-term proposition. The marketplace hasn't really spoken to that short-term minded client who wants to park cash for a period of time and then achieve liquidity and then go do something else. That's not really what Delaware Statutory Trusts and the securitized 1031 market has been about.

"There are certain assets that may be shorter term hold propositions: an asset with shorter term financing that has perhaps a value-add proposition attached to it, probably on the higher risk side of the spectrum, but it could also be higher upside in the shorter-term hold.

"Inland has done a concept of five-year type structures. Those are more few and far between... When I explain our marketplace to people, I find using the baseball analogy [helpful]: 90% of our investors have done really well by themselves by investing actively in real estate, buying and selling, actively owning and managing their own property, and its's that point in their lives where they no longer want to be active owners, but they like real estate, they believe in it, and they obviously are tax sensitive. So, they roll their proceeds out of an actively-managed property into a passive one. And they've already swung for the fences, they've already hit their homeruns, they've already accumulated a great deal of wealth and by the time they get to our industry, our marketplace, they're looking to hit consistent singles, they're looking to preserve capital, they're looking to put their money to work for them in the form of income. Because of that, a long-term mind set it makes sense."

IS THERE A CASH RESERVE FACTOR BUILT IN?

"Always, always. In fact, I preach this internally, but we go to great pains to err on the side of making sure there's even more than we believe we're going to need because the real estate industry is dynamic and you can never completely predict exactly what's going to occur. There always are surprises, some pleasant, some unpleasant, so you're better served having more cash set aside just in case."

AT TAX TIME, WHAT SORT OF FORMS DO INVESTORS GET?

"If it's a DST, it's a 1099 which is a pretty simple document. It's a summary of the property level income and expenses; shows the net income translated to investors who use that to fill out schedule E on their tax return. That's a process most of our investors are familiar with because that's how they filed for their prior holdings. The difference is, with a DST it's all very clean, broken out and presented in a simple digestible form that most accountants can navigate pretty efficiently."

There's a perception that investors are taking their money out of multi-family units in California.

"In our industry we're still seeing the largest percentage of influx still going into apartments. Now there's certainly some geographic considerations. I think in California, for example, pricing dynamics are a bit more of an outlier when compared to national averages. So, we do see a lot of inflow of capital coming from the respective coasts and a lot of times those investors are observing: I can sell my property for a value that is well above what I ever thought I would get, and I can redeploy that capital into another market, a similar asset, a multi-family dwelling in a different market that maybe has more in the way of income producing potential and upside potential. That's kind of dependent on the particular market but apartments consistently are the leading sector that 1031 investors in our industry are allocating capital to. That's at the moment. That tide can absolutely change."

What about the Amazon Effect?

"It goes back to that discussion we had earlier about technology...Inland in its retail strategy has for several years now really dedicated its pursuit of new opportunities and isolated them into grocery-anchored facilities and facilities that have a large concentration in service-related [establishments]: nail salons, and haircuts and establishments that can't be bought online.

"It was a hedge against the online phenomenon, but even taking that approach doesn't isolate you, doesn't make you immune to what's going on and how retailers are impacted. Retailers conclude that maybe they need less space than before. We've seen it already this year with Sports Authority, for example. Retailers are put out of business as a result. What that's creating is more available space which translates into downward pressure on rents which can affect your values. I think the retail industry will emerge and kind of process its way through the Amazon Effect, and long term, I think buying a well-located shopping center and having a long-term mindset can make a high degree of sense. But it's definitely an inflection point for that particular sector, and one you really need to navigate with caution."

THERE CERTAINLY ARE OTHER FORMIDABLE DST SPONSORS

Yes, Inland stands above the rest of the DST sponsors in capital raise numbers but it would not be fair not to mention others. There are seven or eight formidable newcomers to the field, that are snapping at the heels of Inland.

EXCHANGERIGHT
INTERVIEW WITH
WARREN THOMAS,
FOUNDING PARTNER

ExchangeRight of Pasadena, California, is the third largest provider of DSTs in the industry, with more than $1.2 billion of property under management.

The company was formed in 2012 in the aftermath of the Great Recession. Founders Warren Thomas, Joshua Ungerecht, and David Fisher had the idea of creating a 1031 Exchangeable product for investors that would withstand the next inevitable downturn in the economy. Their philosophy is to protect their investors' capital and the stability of their income.

Geoff Flahardy, an icon in the industry, was working at another real estate company during the recession. When he heard about ExchangeRight and its philosophy, he joined the company to help build out its DST platform.

I consider Geoff a real pioneer in the DST industry as well. His dedication to the industry, the investors, and to representatives such as myself is truly unmatched and honorable. His dedication is of the highest standard. And this doesn't even touch upon his amazing math skills; he can figure out complicated transactions in no time flat and does so on short notice with investors on a conference call. Quite amazing really! He is known for his straight talk and is never in a selling mode. Just the facts ma'am.

Geoff was finishing work on his college degree in Organizational Communication when he posted his resume on a jobs board. He was hired as an intern in 2001 and hired full-time six months later. When the company launched a subsidiary to offer Tenant-in-Common investments, Geoff became one of the specialists in 1031 Exchanges.

As with other DST issuers, ExchangeRight follows a number of detailed steps in forming the Trust, Private Placement Management creation, getting third party tax opinion and so forth.

In one of the strategies and asset classes, Geoff took notice of corporate NNN properties that held up well in 2008-2010. We asked Warren Thomas of ExchangeRight why they do what they do: Listen up! This guy is fascinating!

WHY DID YOU FORM EXCHANGERIGHT SECURITIES, LLC IN 2012?

"The founding partners of ExchangeRight formed the company to meet the needs of their personal investors who were seeking to complete 1031 Exchanges and desired property assets that could preserve capital and deliver reliable monthly income, regardless of the economic conditions that might accompany a recession or economic turmoil. ExchangeRight introduced the 1031 DST industry to multi-property portfolios of net-leased assets with long-term leases guaranteed by investment grade corporation. The ExchangeRight model incorporated the use of modest levels of debt with high to very high debt-service coverage ratios, to protect the investor and the portfolio from defaults and risk of foreclosure. ExchangeRight also introduced the concept of waiving certain disposition fees while providing a strategically planned exit of aggregated portfolios. The result of this model was that ExchangeRight has issued 22 net leased portfolios, all with returns meeting or exceeding original projections and now manages total assets of $1.3B."

IN BOTH THE INVESTMENT AND EXIT STRATEGY, WHY IS EXCHANGERIGHT TAKING THE CURRENT APPROACH?

"We have taken the approach of building portfolios of net leased assets that have been first and foremost generating consistent cash flow with little to no risk of losing capital due to debt structure that could result in future foreclosure risk. Secondly, we are targeting future exits that allow our portfolios to be aggregated and command a premium through sales to institutional and high net worth buyers. We are quite pleased that our portfolio approach has resulted in each DST meeting or exceeding original projections in their operations. We are also very encouraged in our early talks with our investment bankers on our future DST exits."

WHY IS EXCHANGERIGHT FOCUSED ON RETAIL ASSETS?

"ExchangeRight is focused on retail net leased assets that we expect to perform well in challenging economic conditions. These types of assets have experienced strong retail performance during the prior recession and we expect them to do the same should economic conditions worsen. We buy the assets we buy because they are naturally defensive in nature because of the products and markets they serve as well as because of the credit of the corporations that tenant the properties."

ARE YOU CONCERNED ABOUT THE AMAZON EFFECT?

"We watch for the Amazon Effect with every asset type that we purchase. Although we are always concerned, we concentrate on necessity-based retail asset types that have thus far had very little impact from Amazon. Auto part retailers, medical providers, pharmacy, dollar stores, Tractor Supply, banks and our other specialized retailers have gained market shares often because of their focus on discount and necessity items that are not as easily or a timely available from Amazon."

WHAT IS YOUR OUTLOOK FOR THE ECONOMY AND REAL ESTATE MARKETS?

"We are hopeful that current tax, economic and regulatory policies will continue to prolong economic growth, but we know the economy is overdue for both a correction and recession. Recession will challenge both occupancies and rent levels of many real estate asset types. Therefore, we continue to acquire net lease assets with investment grade tenants that we expect will perform well in a recessionary environment. We also will continue to seek multifamily assets, but we will only acquire those assets that have a significant value add component which can assist the property to retain and increase in value during tough economic times."

CANTOR FITZGERALD

Cantor Fitzgerald is a global financial services firm. It has been around since 1945, and it and its affiliates have ten thousand employees in 60 offices in 20 countries spread around the globe.

Cantor Fitzgerald lost 658 employees in the September 11, 2001, terrorist attack in New York City. CEO Howard Lutnick vowed to keep the company alive, and it was able to bring its trading markets back online within a week. The company also vowed to give 25% of its profits over the next five years to the families of the employees who were killed.

Cantor Fitzgerald did $56 billion dollars' worth of real estate transactions in 2017. It is an industry leader in multi-family financing for Fannie Mae, Freddie Mac and the F.H.A.

Cantor Fitzgerald's DST business comprises single-tenant and multi-family properties. We can go on for several pages, but why don't you settle in and watch their video or check them out on line. www.cantor.com

Accommodator's Perspective, your 1031 Exchange Escrow: Interview with William Exeter, President & CEO Exeter 1031 Exchange Service

I sat down with one of the leaders in the 1031 Exchange space: Bill Exeter. William L. Exeter is President and Chief Executive Officer for Exeter 1031 Exchange Services, LLC, Exeter IRA Services, LLC and their affiliate companies.

Building and Maintaining Wealth

"Real estate investors spend a lifetime buying, building and managing their investment real estate portfolio, but they rarely consider what they will do once they get to the point where they are "done" with managing their investment real estate.

"The sale of investment real estate will generally result in the recognition of federal and state ordinary income, capital gain and/or depreciation recapture tax liabilities. It may also trigger the Medicare ("Obamacare") Surcharge. The combined federal and state income tax paid can easily approach 40% of the investor's taxable gain.

"Payment of these income tax liabilities will significantly reduce the amount of equity (cash) available to reinvest in other rental, investment or business use properties thus making it extremely difficult for an investor to continue building his or her wealth.

"Investors are often very good at building and creating wealth through the accumulation of an investment real estate portfolio, but keeping that wealth is just as important as building it. Why work so hard to build your wealth if you lose a large percentage of that wealth to taxes?"

PLANNING YOUR EXIT STRATEGY

"Investors, in conjunction with their legal, tax and financial advisors, should start planning as early as possible for their 'exit strategy' by answering questions such as: Do I want to change my investment real estate portfolio in any way? Do I need more cash flow instead of appreciation for my retirement? Do I want to reduce the amount of time that I spend on property management activities? Do I want to spend my wealth or leave it to my kids and/or grandkids? There are many other factors that an investor may want to consider when contemplating an exit strategy, which is why working with legal, tax and financial advisors is exceptionally important.

"Tax deferral strategies can effectively allow an investor to reposition or rebalance his/her investment real estate portfolio to accomplish any number of financial, tax or estate planning goals and objectives while deferring the payment of federal, and in most cases, state income tax liabilities.

"One of the most popular tax-deferral strategies today is the tax-deferred exchange pursuant to Section 1031 of the Internal Revenue Code ("1031 Exchange")."

1031 EXCHANGE

"The 1031 Exchange allows an investor to sell appreciated rental, investment or business use real estate and defer the payment of income tax liabilities as long as he/she remains fully invested by acquiring Qualified Use and like-kind replacement real estate of equal or greater value.

"Structuring a 1031 Exchange is certainly an excellent transaction tool for deferring the payment of taxes when an investor sells rental or investment real estate. However, the 1031 Exchange is much, much more than just a transaction tool. It is an incredible wealth building opportunity. It allows the investor to continually defer the payment of capital gain and depreciation recapture income tax liabilities over his/her lifetime. This means that investors can continue exchanging properties as a life-long strategy, always deferring the payment of their income tax liabilities and keeping their equity (cash) working for them. This strategy allows investors to significantly increase the value of their investment real estate portfolio and consequently their net worth over their lifetime.

"It can also be a tax elimination strategy. An investor can continually defer the payment of income tax liabilities through a life-long 1031 Exchange strategy, and then leave the investment real estate to heirs who will receive a step-up and cost basis thereby completely eliminating the payment of any capital gain and depreciation recapture taxes."

QUALIFIED INTERMEDIARY

"You will need a professional, experienced, knowledgeable and financially sound Qualified Intermediary like Exeter 1031 Exchange Services, LLC to structure your 1031 Exchange transaction. The Qualified Intermediary is responsible for the administration of your 1031 Exchange transaction, including (1) preparation of your 1031 Exchange documents; and, (2) safeguarding your 1031 Exchange funds; and (3) consulting with you and your advisors regarding the implementation of your 1031 Exchange transaction."

Qualified Use Requirement

"One of the most important issues regarding 1031 Exchanges is the Qualified Use requirement. In other words, what types of property qualify for 1031 Exchange treatment?

"Investors often get hung up on how long they have held or will hold title to real estate in order to determine if they qualify for 1031 Exchange treatment. There is no holding period requirement. The actual requirement is that under audit the investor must be able to demonstrate the intent to hold the relinquished property and their replacement property for rental, investment or business use.

"The longer the investor holds the subject properties for investment purposes the easier it is to prove the intent was to hold for rental, investment or business use. However, if an investor has a short-term holding period he might still be able to qualify if he can satisfactorily demonstrate that he did have the intent to hold but there were either business, economic or other reasons for the short-term hold.

"Property held for sale by rehabbers, flippers, developers, and building contractors generally will not qualify for 1031 Exchange treatment because they bought the property with the intent to rehab, improve or build and then sell. It is treated as inventory in their real estate business. Property acquired for personal use such as your primary residence, second home or vacation property will not qualify unless changes are made regarding the usage of the property."

LIKE-KIND PROPERTY REQUIREMENT

"There is a lot of misinformation circulating today about the Like-Kind Property requirement. It does not mean that you must buy a condo if you sell a condo. It only means that you are selling real estate and must therefore buy real estate. It is a very broad definition – real estate for real estate – period."

1031 EXCHANGE DEADLINES

"Investors must comply with very specific deadlines in order to qualify for 1031 Exchange treatment, including the 45 calendar-day identification requirement and the 180 calendar-day exchange deadline. These deadlines both start running upon the closing of the sale of the relinquished property. There is no extension available for these deadlines. The 45 calendar-day identification requirement can be very stressful when you are trying to locate and identify property to acquire as part of your 1031 Exchange transaction.

"One of the many benefits of identifying and acquiring a beneficial interest in a Delaware Statutory Trust ("DST") as part of a 1031 Exchange is that you can substantially eliminate the risk of the 45 calendar-day identification period by purchasing and closing on one or more DSTs during the 45 calendar-day period.

"Investors often identify DST investment properties as back-up properties or to be used with any excess 1031 Exchange funds that are left over after the acquisition of their target property."

Identifying Replacement Properties

"Potential replacement properties must be identified to the 1031 Exchange Qualified Intermediary within the 45 calendar-day identification period. The property identification should be specific and must comply with either the three (3) property rule, the 200% of fair market value rule, or the 95% exception. Basically, the three-property rule is to identify no more than 3 replacement properties and close on between one and three of them in the allotted 180 days. Another option is the 200% FMV rule. This rule allows an investor to identify as many properties as they like as long as the combined fair market value of those properties does not exceed 200% of the investors relinquished property sale price. And finally, the 95% rule allows an investor to identify as many properties as they like as long as the investor actually acquires and closes on 95% of them."

Refer to your 1031 escrow company for details or an accommodator. Here are a couple of excellent sources: www.EXETER1031.com www.IPX1031.com.

Reinvestment Requirement

"The value of the replacement properties acquired must be equal to or greater than the value of the relinquished properties sold. In other words, the investor must trade equal or up in value based upon the relinquished property value. You are not just reinvesting the profit or the equity, but the entire value.

"The investor can certainly complete a 'partial 1031 Exchange' by trading down in value and/or pulling some equity (cash) out of the 1031 Exchange transaction, but it will result in the recognition of taxable gain. There is no way to pull cash out without incurring tax consequences.

"You can sell multiple relinquished properties and or acquire multiple replacement properties as part of either a consolidation or a diversification strategy. The DST can be a huge help when investors want to diversify their investment real estate portfolio."

Q&A WITH THE LEADING DST MONEY GUY: CONVERSATION WITH CHARLES JENSEN

Charles Jensen--Senior Vice President Inland Securities Corporation. Charles is called the leading capital raiser on DSTs in the nation and this is what he shared with me on the topic of DSTs.

CHARLES WHY IS THE DST INDUSTRY GROWING, WHAT DO YOU ATTRIBUTE THIS TO?

"I attribute this growth to the demographic changes happening in the United States. When you look at our population and the areas that we are growing in, the Baby Boomer aspect of that group is growing significantly right now; They are 25% of the population. They want the tax benefits of the 1031 Exchange, but they don't want the hassle of the day-to-day management. The Delaware Statutory Trust has many benefits. Some of these benefits are the diversification they get because of the multiple properties inside of one Delaware Statutory Trust. The management is fully taken care of for them so there's no "tenants, toilets, trash, terminal termites, teenagers, taxes" and they get professional management in high-quality properties. The minimum is only $100,000 and just like a typical 1031 Exchange investors are allowed to "swap until they drop" as we say in the industry. The seniors can exchange over and over again, and upon death there's a "step-up in cost basis" to their heirs, [i.e.: they will not have capital gains on the appreciated value.] So, this is a really interesting way to own real estate without the hassles of management.

"To be in high quality properties with a nice income stream some seniors think about creating a charitable trust, but what they can do is look into a Delaware Statutory Trust instead. DSTs send out a monthly income, and also have a growth potential. The person that would like to set up a charitable remainder trust, can instead set up a Delaware Statutory Trust and actually take the income while they're alive. Then upon death, have the income and the property inherited over to the charity with a charitable remainder trust. Instead of giving control over to the charity while alive, being in a Delaware Statutory Trust allows you to remain in control of the asset but not the day-to-day operations. The great thing about the Delaware Statutory Trust is that when it completes and goes full cycle or sells, you have the option of rolling that money into another exchange and starting over again, almost like Groundhog Day."

CHARLES, AS THE INDUSTRY IS NOW MATURED, AND INVESTORS ARE MORE FAMILIAR WITH THE DST CONCEPT, YOU WERE SAYING THAT YOU'RE SEEING VERY LARGE INVESTORS CHOOSING DST FOR THEIR EXCHANGE AS WELL--IS THIS CORRECT?... WHY ARE THE LARGER INVESTORS THAT SEEM TO HAVE OPTIONS, DOING DSTS?

"Just like smaller investors, larger investors have similar goals with regard to retirement. They not only want to retire from their job, but also retire from the management of their properties. Last year in Los Angeles, my average size of a DST was $600,000. [This claim can be made of previous years as well.] I believe the wealthy investors are realizing that the Delaware Statutory Trust is a viable option. Now we're also seeing even larger deals, in the $10-20, $50 million range. Typically, if an investor has over $15 million in equity, we can offer up a customized 1031 Exchange instead of being in the Delaware Statutory Trust with 500 investors. If they have over $15 million they can go into a customized 1031 Exchange through Inland. We are one of the few DST firms in the nation that allows for customized exchanges. This allows the investors to remain in control of the decisions but allows Inland to do the property management on a big asset. The other reason large investors like to work with Delaware Statutory Trusts is the idea of diversification.

"We recently worked with a very wealthy group of families in a trust in Hawaii. They had many properties destroyed by hurricanes in the 1990s which affected the cash flow on their trust. They decided it would be best to convert certain properties into a Delaware Statutory Trust on the mainland managed by Inland. They now have diversification from geographical issues such as hurricanes, and higher quality properties with professional management from Inland with very little day-to-day operations at all on the properties. There's no management they have to spend time on, they're also getting a higher cash flow than they were receiving on the Hawaiian Islands. In addition, they are getting a lower "property management see-through." Inland is diversified into multiple states and multiple asset classes. For example, they were getting charged 12% on the rents on their properties in the Hawaiian Islands, and Inland is only charging 3% on the rents anyway so not only did the property management fee go down drastically, but their income went up as well.

"One of the interesting things about a 1031 Exchange is the fact that if you have a million-dollar property you need to replace a million dollars in real estate to be fully tax-deferred. Now if you have a property that has leverage this gets a little more complicated, so if you had a million-dollar property and it was $500,000 in debt and $500,000 in equity you have a 50% loan to value. When you sold this property the $500,000 in debt was paid back to the original bank regional loan, thus leaving you with $500,000 in proceeds. But the issue is $500,000 does not replace the full million on the replacement property. This requires individuals to get another loan for the $500,000 or to come out of pocket with the $500,000 to replace the debt. The problem is that most investors don't have $500,000 laying around so they are forced to get another loan to replace the debt in a DST. With the allowed up to 500 investors, it is too difficult to get 500 people approved for a loan, so we take out one loan on the property and investors absorb our debt. Some of our deals have zero debt; some have 50% loan to value; and some have 60% loan to value or higher. The fact that you don't need to get another loan simplifies the process. One of the important things to realize in a Delaware Statutory Trust is that all the properties are pre-closed and pre-financed and all due diligence is completed in advance for us, making it turn key to the investor.

"This turn key solution is almost like picking out items from a menu at a restaurant, you can look at the different DSTs to see which ones matches your objectives. Choose between one company or many or pre-select the best of three.

"Our acquisitions process is very robust, we look at many states. We look at states that are growing, industries that are growing, and we try to focus on areas that provide necessities in the market such as apartments, storage units. In medical facilities we looked through hundreds and literally thousands of properties to find that one property to go into the DST. Sometimes if you go to your local realtor or commercial real estate broker, they farm a certain area of town. For example, if you go to San Diego they'll show you San Diego properties in San Diego markets such as Temecula. Typically, that local broker will not show you a national portfolio. But Inland is practically looking at properties in almost every state in the nation, and we like states that are the path of growth."

TELL US ABOUT SOME OF THE OTHER MAJOR REWARDS IN DEALING WITH DSTs THAT YOU'VE EXPERIENCED.

"Clearly the Delaware Statutory Trust is not for everyone, but for the people that this does fit, it's an amazing experience. I have met with investors who own multiple apartment buildings and have done all the management themselves; to see the stress in their faces and hear it in their voices is heartbreaking. I've had some closing dinners months after the investor has invested in a DST. To see their face, and how they look now...; they are in a state of tranquility because their tenants are no longer calling them about a water heater or an issue in the middle of the night. Many are rested and seem able to have a higher quality of life. Nothing makes me happier than helping people realize their goals objectives and live a better life.

"We have begun working with a lot of commercial brokers and residential real estate agents. We have realized there's a lot of synergies between what we do and what they do. Sometimes an investor is retired and doesn't have an income, so he or she can't qualify for a loan. Or sometimes an investor's credit is hurt from a divorce or some life event. The Delaware Statutory Trust doesn't require a credit score for the investor because Inland provides the debt and Inland Services the debt. So, when many realtors or commercial brokers have a situation where the investor is turned down for financing on their 1031 Exchange, they can turn to the financial advisor for the financing through the DST. Not only to replace the debt, but also under the three- property rule the realtor can put it on his property as #2 and 3, as a backup behind the real estate broker. Or they can work in coordination with a Delaware Statutory Trust and a real piece of property. The Delaware Statutory Trust has allowed many realtors to get many more listings because we're bringing this solution to the table. To the aging Baby Boomers and many others in addition, the DST provides properties that are off market to realtors, thus allowing investors a larger choice of properties nationwide."

WE SAVED THE BEST FOR LAST! FORMER PRICEWATERHOUSECOOPER SENIOR CORPORATE AUDITOR/CPA "VOICE OF THE INDUSTRY" MARK KOSANKE

Let me introduce you to the early pioneer of the DST industry: Mark Kosanke, CPA

-- The former PricewaterhouseCooper Senior Corporate Auditor, who was instrumental in creating the first trade association now called ADISA. He is past president and board member. In my opinion, Kosanke was a great 'get' for this book, as he is widely thought of and respected as the voice of this industry. It is my hope that you the reader, if you don't have already, will now get a laser focused understanding of just exactly what a DST will do for you, your life style, your business, and your legacy. I now give you Mark Kosanke:

"As a CPA, what I am telling clients about 1031/DSTs...

"Bob Seger, one of my favorite artists, has a song called "The Famous Final Scene". Perhaps he wasn't speaking about death but a 1031 Exchange strategy. For years tax accountants, investments advisors and CPAs have encouraged their clients to utilize their employers' 401k, 403b, IRAs and other tax deferred accounts. They are great tools. but with one caveat. Someday someone will pay tax on the monies in those funds. They will pay tax on all the money contributed along with all the growth earned over the years. So, whether it is the contributor paying on his/her own withdrawals, or beneficiaries paying on inherited qualified money, the tax will get paid someday.

So how is a 1031 Exchange different? A 1031 allows for deferral of the gain today. Much like an IRA allows for the deferral today of current income. But subsequent 1031s allow for continued deferral, and another, and another until, I like to say, that you have maximized your tax deferral strategy. How do you maximize the strategy? You die! That's right. Die. The adage in our business is 'swap until you drop!' So, what happens after I drop?

"An IRA and a 1031 Exchange operate very differently from a tax standpoint. In an IRA, our beneficiaries inherit our qualified funds and the associated taxes on them. In the case of inherited assets, like real estate and stocks, the rules are entirely different. Our beneficiaries (spouses, children, significant others) inherit those assets from us at the fair market value on the date of our death. So, while you as the deferring party may have little to no tax basis, and therefore huge gains, the beneficiaries' basis becomes market value on the date of death. Sale immediately following death results in no tax! The deferred tax goes "poof" on the exchanger's last breath.

"For example, say you have a property worth $1M with a $100,000 basis. You have a $900,000 taxable gain. If you sell the property on Friday and do not complete a 1031 Exchange, you will owe taxes on the entire gain, a roughly $200,000 tax bill depending on the state you live in. If instead you die on Thursday night before closing, and your children sell the property following Monday's funeral, they have zero taxes to pay. Why? Because their tax basis "stepped up" when you died. Their tax basis is $1M. Their sale is completely tax free. The entire tax bill went "poof"!

"So, if you are someone who has been utilizing an IRA, 401k, 403b or other similar account to defer taxes you should view a 1031 Exchange as the ultimate tax deferral tool. Qualified accounts on steroids. And one of the best wealth transferring tools there is. It's a final scene worth planning for!"

The final scene as reality.

"I work with a lot of clients who feel their final scene is always a-long-ways away. They manage their properties, work with the tenants, the contractors, the leasing agents, the local authorities. They have it down. They are maximizing the income and value of the real estate. Their spouse or children on the other hand are clueless. If all of a sudden, because of death, the management of the properties fell into their laps it would be chaos. In many cases the properties are sold by surviving beneficiaries at bargain prices because a) they just want the cash, b) they have no idea how to manage the property, c) they live out of the area and don't want to be bothered, or d) have no clue what the real value of the real estate is. I've seen many examples where a hardworking, dedicated owner passes away unexpectedly. The resulting sales are a fraction of what that aging owner could have sold those properties for if he had committed to an orderly sale, maximizing their values, and exchanging into a professionally managed, high quality real estate, providing market income without the worry of management."

A better Curtain-call.

"Sometimes the hardest part for personal owners/ managers of real estate is letting go. Most of these entrepreneurs have been accumulating, developing, and managing for decades. It's just not in their DNA to stop. In the end, the reality is that what has been built over those long hard years of work is best retained and passed on to future generations by letting go. Letting go and putting the future in the hands of a nationally-experienced, industry-dedicated professional team. By planning and executing an orderly transition to these real estate professionals the sweat equity of years is retained, and more importantly, passed on to their heirs, tax free using the 1031 Exchange.

"One of the objections to this approach is the "I don't need a partner." 'I don't need a partner.' Individual owners look at various exit strategies involving multiple co-owners, like a Delaware Statutory Trust (DST), as a threat to their style, an added burden of dealing with other people, a loss of control. While that is one side of the equation the other side is much more important. The other side is a national real estate company, encompassing in some cases billions of dollars in real estate, and looking to maximize owner value at every turn. The properties bought through a DST are far superior than what the average investor is ever going to have the chance to afford or buy. The tenants will be bigger, stronger, more credit worthy that anything an individual investor can hope for. The properties most likely are newer and better located. In some cases multiple properties will be combined into one DST offering greater diversification than an individual could ever hope for. The DST sponsor also handles all the communication. There is generally no dealings ever with the other co-owners (beneficiaries) in the DST. You may not want a partner, but if that partner has expertise and reaches far beyond your own doesn't it make sense let them do what they do best.

"The DST sponsors are charged with the task of providing monthly "mailbox" income that can be relied upon by you in retirement. Ultimately, upon your passing, your beneficiaries continue to enjoy that same monthly income that continues to flow without any effort on their part. What a passing gift that is. Your wife, your children, continue to get the same income you were generating without the need to deal with the toilets, the tenants, or the trash. It's a curtain call that deserves a bow as you have provided the ultimate performance for your loved one!

"I have a 76-year-old client who has been 'hands on' in managing 24 beautiful single-family rentals. He meticulously maintains them, handles the tenants, deals with the city inspectors, and works with the various contractors. His wife has never even seen the inside of half of the properties even though they are all within 30 minutes of their residence. His two daughters live in other States. He nets about 2% cash flow on the value of the assets. If something untimely were to happen to him what do you suppose would happen to the real estate? Most likely his wife/daughters would liquidate, stopping the flow of income. How long would that take? Perhaps years. And without personal knowledge of the real estate, perhaps at sale prices below true value. Smartly, this client has been slowly selling and transitioning these properties, via a 1031 Exchange and DST, into "mailbox" income that his wife and daughter can enjoy beyond his curtain call."

Hey Good Lookin

"'Hey good looking, watcha got cookin?' So says Jimmy Buffet. Well who are these DST sponsors and why should we trust them with our lifetime of accumulated wealth?

These are companies like Inland Private Capital, who you've read about in other places in this book. Companies with a national presence. Companies with entire acquisition and disposition departments. Companies with insurance departments, property tax appeal departments, and management departments. Companies that look at 100 properties before buying one. There is no doubt that investing in a DST with one of these sponsors will mean you will have a better property, better tenant, better location, and more upside than anything you could ever buy on your own. The depth and experience of their nationally staffed departments is unapparelled. Imagine taking your local knowledge and spreading it across the entire country. That's what you are getting with a DST sponsor. Imagine a whole department dedicated to reducing taxes, reducing loan rates, competitively bidding out services, negotiating leases. Why buy local when you can buy, via a DST, into the strongest growing market in the country. In a state where there may be no state or local taxes. In a state where demand is growing. In a new property with no barriers to entry to the locale. The average individual investor just can't touch the kind of real estate offered in a DST.

"DSTs offer extremely competitive, on a net return basis, returns. In my experience, most clients think they are getting an 8-10% return on their assets. In reality, with few exceptions, the total net return I see on many tax returns is far less and averages about 3% on true net value. DSTs by comparison offer a far more CONSISTENT return at a higher overall rate. And without the worry of management. A good lookin return!

"DSTs offer so much more. The typical investor has some level of debt on their property. In most cases that debt carries personal guarantees. Can the individual investor hope to negotiate the same debt terms as a national DST sponsor? DSTs offers investors the benefit of no personal guarantees. No credit checks. No tax returns, financial statements, no reporting. This is a strong estate planning tool as well.

"What if there is no debt? Should a seller/exchanger consider adding debt before sale? Absolutely. Debt, and therefore equity, taken out before an exchange is tax free. Debt properly structured prior to a sale allows the seller to extract equity, tax free, prior to sale. Most DSTs offer 45-55% debt leverage. By matching, or closely matching, the ending debt, the seller is able to take out equity tax free before a sale or exchange."

THIS MAKES THE COMBINATION OF A DST AND A PRE-DEBT EXTRACTION THE MOST POWERFUL TOOL IN THE 1031 EXCHANGE HANDBOOK."

"Most investors have used refinancing over the years to maximize their real estate purchases. A DST is no different. DSTs provide the debt typically needed to complete a 1031 Exchange under IRS rules. In some cases, it provides more debt than is needed. In those cases, the opportunity exists to use the DST's non-recourse debt to take out tax free equity 'locked in' our properties. Just another example of making DSTs 'good looking!!'

"Let's look at another example. Suppose my property is worth a $1M. I have about $250K (25%) of personally guaranteed debt on it. The DST I am considering is 55% leveraged. I can go and borrow 25-30% of new debt prior to sale to 'equalize' the approximate debt of the relinquished property with the replacement property. In this way I take out $250-$300K tax free before my sale. As long as I am using those funds for business or investment purposes The IRS allows this in the normal course of business."

YOU'RE MY BEST FRIEND

"The rock group Queen had a song in the 80s called 'You're My Best Friend.' So, what is the best friend of real estate investors? Depreciation! That's right. That

IRS rule that allows us to offset our cash income with a non-cash deduction call depreciation. And when you combine depreciation with the tax deferring attributes of a 1031 Exchange the affect is mind blowing.

"Let's take a closer look at depreciation and a 1031. If I buy an apartment building for $1M I can depreciate it for 27.5 years. That means, for tax purposes, I get to deduct about $36,000+ off my cash income each year. My property produces $50,000 of income after expenses. After deducting $36K in depreciation I pay tax on only $14K of income. A great tax sheltering reason for owning investment real estate. Now suppose I sell that property after 10 years and do not complete a 1031 Exchange. Under current tax rules I owe what's called 'recapture tax' on the $360,000 in total depreciation I took over the 10 years. I would owe $90,000 in recapture tax even if the property had not appreciated in value. It's basically the IRS saying you got to take that deduction each year, but your property didn't really depreciate, so you owe us the tax back on all those depreciation deductions you took. Recapture tax is 25% of the depreciation previously taken. This is also a major item that many investors do not take into account when 'ball parking' the tax they'll owe if they sell their property and do not complete a 1031.

"When completing a 1031 Exchange that recapture tax is not paid. And if you swap again, it's not paid again. Again and again until death you depart. In the end, with proper planning, that recapture tax is never paid and all those deductions you took over all those years remain tax sheltered income to you for life. Just like your best friend for life!

"How can a DST help me maximize my depreciation deduction and overall income sheltering? DSTs carry leverage ranging from 0% - 80% leverage. The average is around 50% but let's look at some tax planning here. If I sell my $1M property that has 30% leverage (debt) I net $700,000 in equity proceeds to exchange. If I go into an average DST with average leverage of 50%, my $700,000 buys $1.4M of new real estate. I just bought $400,000 more in real estate then I sold. I get to depreciate $400,000 more in 'additional' real estate. I just created $10-$14K more in depreciation to tax shelter my income than I had before. Even if my cash flow is the same I just increased my true after-tax return by sheltering more of the income with depreciation. And, if planned properly, I will never pay tax on that additional depreciation that I am deducting each year I own my DST. This is where utilizing the DST leverage properly can create even more after-tax income than I could ever hope to create on my own.

"In comparing DSTs you can't just look at first year cash flow. This is a mistake many investors make. You have to consider the amount of leverage. You also have to consider the type of property and the amount of depreciation that it will create. Debt reduction and amortization are also key components to consider when comparing various DSTs.

"The ability of the DST sponsors to structure competitive debt and perform depreciation maximizing cost segregation analysis is far above even the most, savvy real estate investor."

"HOW DO I KNOW IF HE REALLY LOVES ME?"

"There are a myriad of DST sponsors out there. How do I know which one is right for me? Which one has my best interest in mind? Which one will be here through good times, and in tough times? Who is just trying to make a quick buck?

"The first thing to understand is federal securities law. Basically, anytime more than a few (often defined as 5) are joined in a profit-making venture requiring the raising of capital, the sale of interest (capital) comes under federal securities law. Those laws outline that a Private Placement Memorandum (PPM) should be created and filed with the Securities and Exchange office (SEC). Further, in these cases, you are now selling a 'security' and by certain disclosure rules. Unfortunately, in the real estate world this is seldom followed and hard to police. There are many examples all over the internet of companies selling "interest" in real estate that has not gone through the registration process with the SEC. And since the SEC only has enough staff to investigate complaints the violations continue unabated.

"Enter your Registered Investment Advisor. Investment advisors are licensed advisors who only deal with DSTs that have taken the care to go through proper channels and scrutiny. Advisors are further licensed through a "Broker/Dealer". For example, a real estate agent has to be licensed through a Broker. If I am a real estate agent I am licensed through Century 21, Remax, or any other Broker. Investment advisors have to be similarly licensed through a Securities Broker/Dealer. The big names you hear are Raymond James, Schwab, Merrill Lynch and others. Most independent advisors specializing in the 1031 arena are licensed with smaller Broker/Dealers that specialize in this area. Broker/Dealers bring an important function to the DST process. As DST sponsors "offer" their programs and products out to the investment world, the Broker/Dealer assumes the role of gatekeeper. It is the responsibility of the Broker/Dealer to review each and every DST presented to them. Only after a thorough review, and the satisfaction of questions or concerns, does a Broker/Dealer sign a 'selling agreement' whereby it begins to allow its licensed investment representatives to offer those DST programs to their clients. This is a huge and very important piece of investing in a DST. The scrutiny that goes into each program is far above the non-securitized transaction being pushed on the internet. There are also very active third party 'due diligence' firms that provide independent reports to the Broker/Dealer community on each program. These affiliate firms provide a valuable service in highlighting potential issues and mitigating attributes within the DST.

"In the end, the DST that your investment advisor is offering to retail clients has been reviewed by multiple independent third party due diligence firms, has been further scrutinized by the Broker/Dealers Due diligence officer, and finally reviewed as appropriate for you, the investing client. This is a far more, lengthy and involved process then any non-securitized offering can provide.

"The result of all this effort is that your independent advisor is presenting to you DST 1031 programs that have gone through an exhaustive process to assure, as best they can, that what you are investing in is a viable offering that meets your needs and protects you as an investor."

"R-E-S-P-E-C-T; Gladys Knight sings. In this this industry who brings this all together to get the RESPECT for the time, effort and talent that goes into making this industry great. The answer – ADISA. ADISA is the Alternative and Direct Investment Securities Association. This is an association made up of the top sponsors, due diligence firms, broker dealers and representatives in the industry. This cohesive group takes the investors interest to the next level. ADISA's primary role is representing the Alternative Investment Industry and providing education, networking, and advocacy. ADISA holds three major conferences each year. These conferences provide a place to properly educate the investment professional, through a series of sessions, specifically aimed at various topics relevant to the products represented. It gives everyone in the industry a chance to network amongst peers to create better products, flow of information, and provide open discussion of industry "best practices."

"ADISA is also actively involved in monitoring new legislation that may impact the alternative investment industry. This is particularly important in tax saving vehicles like the 1031 exchange, which are constantly viewed as a potential revenue source by Congress. Since the advent of the 1031 exchange in 1921 the code has only been modified 6 times, and many of those modifications enhanced the ability to utilize 1031 exchanges. A recent example is that personal property assets starting in 2018 are no longer eligible for 1031 exchanges. This is part of the new tax law. During those Congressional discussions ADISA, along with other real estate trade groups, actively lobbied and educated members as to the benefits of keeping 1031 for real estate in place. As a result, 1031 exchanges for real estate was retained while 1031 exchanges for other non-real assets were not. This was a great example of how this industry stays ahead of the curve in protecting the industry and its investors. Know that ADISA will continue to be a strong voice representing the interest of taxpayers and the industry alike."

"**Easy like Sunday Morning!** That's what reporting a 1031 exchange on your tax return is. As a CPA I appreciate the fact that 1031 exchanges are definitely not an everyday strategy that is used by most of our clients. For that reason, many accountants discount the use of a

1031 merely because they haven't been exposed to it and feel the reporting is complex. In reality the reporting of a 1031 exchange is no more difficult than most other taxable transactions on a tax return."

"There are two pieces to consider here. First there is the 1031 exchange itself which is reported one time, in the year of the exchange. The reporting is similar to reporting capital gains with the caveat that the gain is being "deferred" to future years. Think of it as a carryforward if you will. And tax returns are filled with carryforward items from instalment sales, charitable contributions, capital losses, etc. Once reported the "deferred gain" is set unless or until a subsequent sale is completed and a 1031 exchange is not utilized."

"Secondly there is the reporting of the DST income. When investing in a DST the end result is that I am a "beneficial owner" of the DST. The IRS considers the DST to be a "pass through" entity for tax purposes. What does all that mean? It means I report my DST income in the exact same place I report any rental income property that I have. That place is the Schedule E for individual taxpayers. The sponsors do an excellent job of reporting the total income of the DST properties and then breaking down each beneficial owner's percentages for reporting purposes. Sponsors provide concise, easy to understand year end reports that make the reporting of these income properties extremely efficient."

"The Beach Boys sing "**Wouldn't it be nice**." Well yes it would be. Let's look at some real-life examples of transactions I have been involved in that changed the lives of the people I worked with."

"I had a couple in their mid-60's who were managing a 100+ unit aging apartment complex. They were sweet as can be. And they loved their renters and knew most of them well. So nice and sweet were they that they hardly ever wanted to raise their rents. As a result, they were able to take about $6,000 a month of income from the property. Which they thought was great. But along came a buyer offering them $4M for the property. Because their basis was near zero it also meant nearly a $1M tax bill. Enter the 1031 and a DST. By utilizing the 1031 exchange they we able to put the entire $4M in proceeds to work for them. The DST's they invested in resulted in creating of over $16,000 per month. This was a life changing event for this couple. They were able to retire, substantially increase their net spendable income, and focus on their health. In the first year they bought a second home in Florida and enjoyed the first cruise of their life. Never did they dream that the asset they toiled at could be used to transform their life and now have the opportunity to enjoy their retirement years. It was a great example of stopping yourself, looking at your situation, and realizing that it was time for the asset to work for you and not the other way around."

"This is typical of compassionate, commendable people who manage real estate with emotions instead of for higher profit. This is where the professionalism of the DST sponsors takes away that burden from the individual investor and manages for the highest and best total return."

"Many times, we find that the income we create using the DST exceeds the income the investor was creating on their own. In addition, the quality of the property, location and tenants almost always exceeds the relinquished property. DST owners are participating in properties that they, in most cases, could never have dreamed of investing in on their own.

Another client I was working with had a profitable operating company that included a large portion of real estate in the operations. In his early 60's he had a heart attack and began to realize that the grind of running the business was taking a toll. While selling the business we were able to allocate a significant portion of the sales price to the real estate assets involved. This allowed us to take the maximum amount possible into a 1031 exchange. While he paid some taxes on the business portion of the transaction the bulk of the proceeds were able to be invested into a DST. That DST ended up creating more income than he was traditionally able to draw from his operating company. Another great example of putting the assets to work for you. Through proper planning the allocation of the sale price reduced his tax bill to the lowest possible level while providing the highest possible DST income going forward."

"In the end, most 1031 exchanges into DST's that I have worked on over my career have:

1. Enhanced the Investors Income

2. Heightened the level of property owned

3. Improved the quality of life for investors

4. Simplified Tax returns

5. Reduced overall risk

6. Provided Greater Diversification

7. Assured income will continue after the primary real estate manager has passed on, whereby he has now maximized his tax deferral for good!

Yes. It's nice!"

SHOULD I BUY MY OWN NNN OR A DST?

A retired University of California-San Diego economics professor recently told me that if he knew then what he knows now, he would certainly have put his $2 million investment in DSTs.

He was interested in purchasing a triple net property (NNN--one in which the tenant or lessee agrees to pay maintenance, taxes and insurance), specifically a Kentucky Fried Chicken franchise.

The professor spent hours making a detailed analysis of 40 different KFCs. He even ventured to South Carolina to visit the property in which he was most interested. He went through the process of buying the property and financing part of the purchase.

Six months later, he returned to the property and was disillusioned. He determined that an individual cannot buy a property with the kind of quality that a larger institution can purchase. He called his own purchase a "leftover," what remained after big REIT and DST purchases had been made.

He also bemoaned the kind of lease he had with the franchisee, which pales in comparison to corporate leases.

He told me, "When I think of all the work I did to get one percentage point higher cash flow than a DST, it just doesn't pencil out; the math just simply doesn't work. It would have taken me a couple hours to do the paperwork needed to do a DST and I would have been done with it.

About the Authors

Don Meredith is one of the early pioneers of the DST 1031 Exchange industry with virtually hundreds of exchanges to his credit. He was formerly a financial radio co-host with one of San Diego's oldest radio stations. He became an accomplished oil painter and stage actor and author all after the age of fifty. Don grew up in Maine and migrated west to beautiful San Diego thirty years ago. He fondly talks about Maine: "they have tremendous ethics where I come from! In Maine a handshake means everything."

Don's father is from upstate New York and was an HR guy as far back as he can remember. Always bringing home aptitude tests for Don to do as a child. His mother is from Bath, Maine. His grandfather founded in 1939 a big seafood restaurant/convention center and inn with log cabins for rent that were on the inlet of New Meadows River right down the street from Brunswick Naval Airbase & BIW. Don actually saw John Wayne christen a ship there.

Don says: "I lived close the ocean and to farm land. "I was driving tractors when I was twelve, not a bad childhood I guess."

[A few photographs below-just for fun]:

Don's most recent painting

Don's painting "Vanessa"

Don's interpertation of a Winslow Homer

Left: Don's in <u>Murder by the Book</u> as Edger Alan Poe.

Right: Scrooge, Don: Christmas Present

DON MEREDITH

Jim Benes is a retired journalist. He spent more than forty years as a writer-producer-editor for CBS Newsradio in Chicago. He is the author of *Season of Joy; Chicago Celebrates the Holidays*, which is based on a December feature he has been doing for WBBM Chicago since 1980.

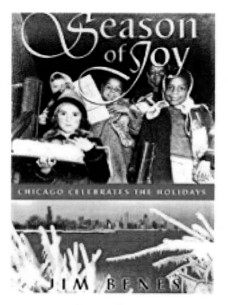

Jim's Book Cover

WA